THE LANDS FORGOTTEN BY TIME

A CRYPTOZOOLOGIST'S GUIDE TO LOST WORLDS AND LEGENDS

BEN TEJADA-INGRAM

Copyright © 2023 by Ben Tejada-Ingram

All rights reserved. No part of this publication may be reproduced, distributed, or transmitted in any form or by any means, including photocopying, recording, or other electronic or mechanical methods, without the prior written permission of the author, except in the case of brief quotations embodied in critical reviews and certain other noncommercial uses permitted by copyright law.

ISBN: 9798857066492

Edited by Miguel Tejada-Flores

Proofread by Carol Ingram

Front cover design by Ben Tejada-Ingram

Title page art by Jirka Houska

All images are copyrighted by the credited photographers or artists, and used in this book with the express permission of the photographers and artists, or are licensed via Unspash.com under the Unsplash License, or are public domain, or designated as CC BY-SA 3.0, CC BY-SA 4.0, or CC-BY-2.5, which are licensed under Creative Commons Attribution Sharealike 3.0 and 4.0, and 2.5 Licenses.

Table of Contents

Foreword 1

Introduction 4

Chapter 1: Domain of the River Stopper 9

Chapter 2: The Archipelago of Fear and Wonder 16

Chapter 3: Sanctuary of the Mountain Yeti 23

Chapter 4: The Oasis of the North 32

Chapter 5: The Lost City of Giants 40

Chapter 6: ....
The Subterranean Realms of the Moon-Eyed People 59

Conclusion 76

About The Author 81

Foreword
By Aleksandar Petakov

The Colorado Rocky Mountains

Photo by Aleksandar Petakov

In 2023, it may seem as though the world has little mystery or intrigue still left in it. We've explored it all, mapped out everything, and have the ability to see into every little corner of the world with high resolution satellite images on Google Earth, with a few clicks online. Even with such resources at our fingertips, in our high tech, fast paced society, most of us simply have no clue how remote parts of the world are. Perhaps even more so now, where more and more people live in urban and suburban areas, and are utterly detached from the vastness of a remote mountain chain or ancient swamplands.

As a self-proclaimed adventurer and filmmaker, I've been beyond fortunate to have traveled across North America and various parts of the world, usually in search of mysterious cryptids such as Sasquatch, mystery big cats or lake monsters, among other things. Whether it be the temperate rainforests of coastal Alaska, to the endless forests of the Appalachians, or vast swamps of the southern US, I've seen firsthand how much space is still out there, waiting to be explored, completely unknown to most people. In fact, I'm often contacted by people who will watch my *Bigfoot: Beyond the Trail* documentary YouTube series, blown away by the natural landscapes and amount of it found on the North American continent. This is not something we are really taught much about anymore, as our ancestors might have been, since it was life or death for them in many cases. Knowledge of these places is something we must seek out ourselves.

When I was approached by the author to write this forward, I immediately was drawn to the idea of this book. Ben's previous literary work on the "little Nessie" of Venezuela sent me into a frenzy of curiosity and research on the topic. This thoughtfully crafted exploration of the lands forgotten by time will almost certainly have you doing your own frenzied research into some of the places Ben chronicles, even if it is at the expense of something else you are supposed to be working on, but it's totally worth it.

In a time where the modern world appears to be closing in on all of us, these lost worlds are a reprieve. Invoking a spirit of the explorers who came before us, whether in search of wealth, mystery creatures or simply natural wonder, Ben will give you a window into some of these mysterious places and the legends that are rumored to lurk in the dark corners of the world.

Sincerely, *Aleksandar Petakov*

www.smalltownmonsters.com

Introduction

The Son Doong Cave of Vietnam

Photo by Daniel Burka

In the early 1990s in a remote jungle in northern Vietnam, something truly incredible happened: scientists began to explore for the first time in the modern age, a real life "Lost World."

The area, known as the *Vu Quang Nature Reserve*, had long been closed off from the western world, due to the fears of the communist regime of Vietnam and the ensuing post-war tensions, but the Reserve had been miraculously spared from the ravages of war. Because of the inhospitable climate, and since the area was both constantly shrouded by mists and subject to torrential rainfalls, it had been a place into which few outsiders had ever ventured for many centuries.

After the Vietnamese government designated the area as a nature reserve and National Park, scientists from within the country and from outside, working under the auspices of the World Wildlife Fund, began to properly explore the region.

In 1992, they made a monumental discovery: the Vu Quang Ox, or Saola, otherwise known fancifully as the "Asian Unicorn," a large, deer-like creature with distinctive horns, which was actually a member of the bovine family. This creature stunned scientists worldwide, as it was the first truly large mammal to be discovered in over 50 years.

The Vu Quang Ox (Saola)

Licensed under CC-BY-SA 3.0, first shared by user Silviculture on the Vietnamese Wikipedia

Then, in 1994, the world was shocked again by the discovery of another animal that was completely new to science, and had never before been seen by the outside world: the Giant Muntjac Deer.

British scientist John MacKinnon described the area as a "lost world that science has never looked at."

The Vu Quang Nature Reserve to date has yielded five new mammal discoveries, which is astonishing due to the rarity of new mammals being discovered, when compared to other types of creatures.

When one ponders the question of how it can be possible for any kind of large, and certainly not inconspicuous creature to remain undiscovered by modern science, one need only to look at the story of the Vu Quang Nature Reserve. The Reserve seems to be a prime example of a "Lost World," where strange, unknown creatures still roam, an area set apart from time and the outside world, so remote that human beings have almost never set foot there to behold its natural wonders.

Additionally, a mere 105 kilometers to the southeast of Vu Quang, another monumental discovery was made in the early 90s: the largest cave in the world, the *Son Doong Cave*. Astonishingly, its discovery was completely accidental, by a local man searching for food in the Phong Nha-Ke Bang National Park. The Son Doong Cave measures an astounding 38.5 million cubic meters according to the latest estimates, and is so immense that its interior possesses its own thriving rainforest ecosystem, complete with its own weather cycles, flora and fauna, including towering trees as tall as buildings, and species of endangered tigers.

As I hope will become apparent through these stories and findings, it is undeniable that real 'lost worlds' do indeed exist, and furthermore, there are many others still awaiting discovery and exploration.

When I finished researching my previous book (*The Last Dinosaur of the Lost World: My Search for 'Little Nessie'*), which contains, among other things, a thorough exploration of a mysterious and actually dubbed "lost world plateau" in a remote corner of Venezuela, I realized I had been (and continue to be!) inspired to discover that such places really did and do exist... wild and mysterious places which have remained largely unexplored by human beings, and which seem filled with their own exciting and as yet hidden discoveries.

It is my intention with this book to further investigate, and hopefully shed a little light on some other so-called "lost worlds" or forgotten lands, in different parts of the world. My lost and forgotten worlds include both physical and real places, where documented reports of strange creatures abound -- and also places considered mythical and legendary, whose existence appears to lie between the bounds of the real and the unknown, lost worlds that still await discovery. My hope is to inspire all those of you who dream of exploring, and who crave adventure -- to ignite the same passion for the unknown that has been a constant in my life, in others. I have found during my own investigations of mysteries that, in the end, what you set out to discover is never as amazing as the people, the characters, or the places that you meet or encounter along the way. In the words of the inimitable explorer and adventurer Josh Gates (who is one of my personal heroes, and is known for hosting the TV program *Expedition Unknown*):

"The true secret to seeking the unknown is in the looking, not the finding. The journey is what matters."

Chapter 1
The Domain of the River Stopper

The Mokele-Mbembe

Illustration by Jirka Houska

In the mist-shrouded heart of Africa's densest, most secluded rainforest, there is a secret. An allegedly prehistoric secret.

Imagine for a moment this all too common tale, that is reported widely. Variations exist, but this amalgamation of the tales contains most of the same key, consistent elements.

As night begins to fall, a fisherman strays too far upriver in his canoe. Searching for the biggest catch, he ventures into what are known to be dangerous waters. As the shadows grow long in the trees, an uneasy silence envelops the normally loud and buzzing jungle. It is as if the animals themselves can sense the forthcoming moment with fear and foreboding.

Then, suddenly, the river ahead starts to churn. A violent disturbance in the waterway sends water flying in all directions. The fisherman, frightened, tries to row away, but it is too late. An enormous beast breaks the surface of the waves, and charges the small boat. The creature roars mightily and thrashes with anger, at this intruder in its domain. The small boat is overturned, and the fisherman is thrown into the water. He manages to swim to shore, and though bruised and shaken, he takes to his heels and flees with the speed of a puny adrenaline-fueled mortal, hoping to outrun his supernatural pursuer, and vowing, as he runs, never to return to this seemingly cursed area.

This scenario, though it may sound far-fetched, is a very common tale in the Congo basin, as well as in parts of east Cameroon. Tales of an enormous, ferocious beast prowling the rivers, have earned this mythical creature a fearsome reputation, as these ferocious beasts are known to attack small boats and canoes. They seem to be fiercely territorial, and the locals are always aware of their lurking menace, and make a point of knowing which areas of the river to avoid.

This fearsome creature is known as the *Mokele-Mbembe*, which translates more or less as, "the stopper of the rivers." Tales of its aggressive nature are as ubiquitous as the many detailed descriptions of its unique appearance. Not to be confused with the hippopotamus, though similar in temperament, the *Mokele-Mbembe* has a distinct appearance. It is always described as being "extremely large," at least the size of an elephant, with short stocky legs, and a long, reptilian tail. However, its most fascinating feature is the long, slender neck, as well as the ridges protruding from both the neck and the spine.

The Mokele-Mbembe, in comparison with a human being.

Drawing by Wikipedia user Amndrkwe, licensed under CC BY-SA 4.0

The area where this creature is said to exist is the second largest tropical rainforest on the planet, second only to the Amazon, and is the largest rainforest on the African continent. The Congo basin itself has always been teeming with wildlife, and it is one of the last largely unexplored wildernesses on earth.

Though inhabited by various tribes and indigenous peoples,

most of this vast jungle region has remained unexplored, due to the denseness of the vegetation and to the generally harsh nature of the jungle environment. Geologically speaking, this area can be thought of as a large basin, roughly the size of Alaska, which sets it apart from both neighboring regions, and from the outside world in general.

When explorers from other countries first ventured into the region, well over 100 years ago, they began immediately hearing the tales of its many strange creatures. It wasn't long until the idea of a relic dinosaur species was proposed.

In the 1980s, Dr. Roy P. Mackal, a biologist from the University of Chicago, began making a series of well publicized expeditions to the Congo with the express purpose of finding or proving the existence of the *Mokele-Mbembe*. The expeditions' members began to gather reports from multiple tribes and indigenous peoples. At this time, as Mackal explored the swampy, sparsely populated region, he was able to collect over 30 different firsthand accounts of the creature from seemingly credible eyewitnesses, from different tribes and varying cultural and ethnic backgrounds. What makes Mackal's findings especially compelling is the fact that many of these tribes and villages had no contact with one another. This suggests that each of the consistent descriptions of what was apparently the same creature, were unique to each group of people giving them, and not likely to have been heard or learned from an outside source. It's important to recognize that the reports were all firsthand -- not ancient tales from the realms of myth, folklore and legend, but detailed accounts given by real, living people who had seen or encountered the beast.

Mackal and his associates conducted a rather unique experiment that has since been replicated by other investigators. In order to rule out known animals, such as elephants, rhinoceroses, hippopotami or the like, he would show the tribesmen illustrations of most of the aforementioned creatures and several others. The inhabitants of these areas were familiar with all of these normal animals, and did not identify any of them as *Mokele-Mbembe*. But, when Mackal showed them an illustration of a sauropod dinosaur (the long-necked, long-tailed, herbivorous type of dinosaur), they would invariably identify the illustrations of sauropods as the *Mokele-Mbembe*.

We need to remember that all of these eyewitnesses did not come from cultures familiar with scientific views or concepts of dinosaurs and paleontology. They were for the most part unfamiliar with the notion of what a dinosaur is, or the fact that most dinosaurs are believed to have been extinct for millions of years. To them, the beast they called a *Mokele-Mbembe* was just another creature living in their immediate environment, one they were familiar with.

In the intervening years, Mackal's experiment has been repeated by other researchers and several such investigations were filmed, during an expedition sponsored by the TV show *Monsterquest* in 2009, and later on the program *Legend Hunter* in 2019.

What other evidence do we have to support the existence of this fascinating but seemingly terrifying creature? Aside from the plethora of eyewitness accounts, there have been a number of strange, 3-toed footprints found over the years along riverbanks. There are a number of intriguing but inconclusive film clips, including one aerial film taken from an airplane by a Japanese research team, which appears to show a large but unidentified mass moving through the water of Lake Tele, which is believed to be the epicenter of the many *Mokele-Mbembe* sightings.

However, when investigating myths and legendary creatures, I believe it is always necessary to interview the local inhabitants, and find out what they have to say. People living in small tribal villages and living off the land, are often intimately familiar with most species of plants and animals in their environment, as a matter of their survival. They need to have the highest degree of knowledge and familiarity with which animals or plants are dangerous, which are benign, and which can be used as food, or for other purposes. They need to know which plants are medicinal, and what natural resources can be used for building or crafting. For all these reasons, I believe it's vital to take these testimonies with the utmost respect and seriousness.

Still, the notion of a living, breathing sauropod dinosaur that survived extinction definitely stretches the limits of credulity and believability, even for those pre-inclined to believe, and certainly for critically-minded explorers. I would like to remind my more skeptical readers that another of the Congo's megafauna, the Gorilla, was thought to be an "invented" folktale, until Gorilla bones and remains were discovered in 1847. Nonetheless, contemporary scientists still scoffed at the notion that these so-called "ape men" might exist, and it wasn't until the beginning of the 20th Century, in 1902, that the first living gorilla specimen was acknowledged by western scientists, and finally recognized as a living creature, and not a fairytale.

In fact, and possibly more pertinent to the subject of this book, as recently as 2008, and in the very same area the *Mokele-Mbembe* is rumored to inhabit, a population of 125,000 western lowlands gorillas was discovered in 2008, in a vast forest swamp region in the Lake Tele reserve. Before this discovery, biologists feared that less than 50,000 western lowlands gorillas still survived. However, in 2006 and 2007, members of the U.S. based Wildlife Conservation Society followed up on tips from local hunters that gorillas had been spotted in this area. After researchers trekked through the jungle for three days, to the outskirts of Lake Tele, they discovered an astonishing number of the primates, the highest density of western lowlands gorillas ever found. After further exploration of the surrounding jungle, they were able to estimate the total gorilla population, based on the density and number of nests found in the area.

It seems to defy all logic, that an enormous population of extremely large animals such as gorillas can remain completely hidden and unknown to the outside world, but this is precisely what occurred in the dense jungles of the Congo basin. And if it's happened once, I'm inclined to believe that discoveries of other endangered species, or hitherto unknown creatures in the same area, are likely to occur again.

The existence of the *Mokele-Mbembe* has some of the strongest firsthand, local testimony of any cryptid on the planet ('cryptid' being the commonly used term for any animal that is not officially recognized by science to exist, or has been classified as extinct). I believe it's just not possible for so many eye-witness accounts to have occurred in the same area without there being *something* out there. Also, we should remember that a basin is a geologically isolated area, and in some ways can be thought of as the geological inverse of a plateau. But potential explorers should be aware that the Congo Basin contains some of the densest, most inhospitable terrain on the planet. It's subject to torrential rainfall, and home to many of the earth's most lethal and dangerous creatures, ranging from minuscule, nearly invisible insects to mighty elephants, and everything in between. The *Mokele-Mbembe* legend is not for the faint-hearted to seek out, but I think it's one of the most promising - and potentially real and true ones - in the world. In fact, the phrase, *"very likely to exist,"* seems like an understatement. I believe wholeheartedly that the *Mokele-Mbembe* is real -- whether it's a surviving dinosaur, or some new species of crocodile, reptile, amphibian or mammal, or some large, semi-aquatic animal. It may still be living in the Congo Basin even as I write these words, still "unknown" to the outside world, awaiting an official "discovery" and verification.

Chapter 2
The Archipelago of Fear and Wonder

A mountainous island in Fiji

Photo by Janis Rozenfelds

In 2020, I was talking to a friend about Bigfoot. I told him a story of an encounter I had growing up. In response, he told me something amazing that made my jaw drop. He said that when he had been growing up in Fiji, he saw a giant bird, that looked almost like a dragon, which swooped down and carried a man away.

As a young child, he had been playing on the edge of a field near a densely forested jungle. He said he witnessed the bird swoop in, grab the man, who had been working in the field, and with it's enormous talons carry him away, as easily as an eagle carrying a mouse. He said the man had screamed, but that no help had come.

Of course, when my friend told the story to his parents, they didn't believe him and told him he must have imagined it. At the time, I honestly didn't know if he had been joking or just messing with me. It took me some time to realize that he had been dead serious about what he told me he had seen - and that he still was.

My friend, who agreed to let me share his story in this book on the condition of anonymity, also told me that he had never told anyone else about this terrifying encounter, because he had come to the conclusion that people would think he was crazy.

As his story seriously intrigued me, I decided it merited further research, and I made up my mind to look into it. But before telling you what I discovered, first we should spend a little time exploring the details of this amazing archipelago nation, made up of 332 separate islands, known as Fiji.

Located in the south Pacific, Fiji possesses a tropical climate, and is considered by many to be a tropical paradise. Fiji is home to approximately 850,000 people, and 87 percent of the population lives on the two "major" islands, Vitu Levu and Vanya Levu. Out of the 332 islands, only 110 are inhabited, leaving the other 222 islands completely devoid of any human presence whatsoever. Many of the islands are mountainous, and a high percentage of the flora and fauna are endemic to Fiji, which essentially means they only live or grow there, and are found nowhere else in the world. Fiji is a biodiversity hotspot, with an abundance of marine species thriving in the diverse habitats of coral reefs, mangrove forests and volcanic rock formations.

While most of Fiji's abundant tourism centers in and around the inhabited islands, its uninhabited islands remain virtually untouched by human beings. These are islands set apart in both time and geographic space from the rest of the world, their secrets and unknown beauty protected by the difficulty of accessing them. They are generally only visited by scientific and/or conservation groups, with rare visits from the occasional ocean-hopping charter vessel.

Common sense suggests it might well be possible for many undiscovered species to live and thrive in the multiple and mysterious habitats of these remote and breathtaking uninhabited islands. But a giant species of unknown bird? The notion still strains the limits of believability.

When I started to research possible connections to my friend's childhood story, initially I hit a dead end. I couldn't find anything. But eventually, I discovered what I had been looking for: the Fijian legend of an animal called the *Ngani-Vatu*.

One of the first known records of this avian beast, usually relegated to the realms of mythology and folklore, can be found in the book "Myths and Legends of the Polynesians" by Johannes Anderson, first published in 1931. Indeed, this book seems to be one of the few real sources of information about the *Ngani-Vatu*, and most subsequent sources seem to be recycling the information from Anderson's book.

The creature he describes exactly fits the bill of what we are looking for: a gigantic predatory bird, with a wingspan of over 15 feet, a fierce disposition, and that has been said to carry away human beings and eat them alive. According to the legends, a fisherman's wife was abducted by the giant eagle (in some versions, the fisherman and wife are demigods). The fisherman sets out on a quest for revenge, and tracks the beast to its lair, which was said to be near *Yasawa* Island. The *Ngani-Vatu* has devoured his bride, and a fierce battle ensues. The fisherman slays the beast with a spear, and uses its giant feathers on his boat as sails, to help catch the wind as he returns home.

Surely all of this is purely imagination, and has no basis in reality, right? But I contend that if we examine this legend from a different perspective, what may be the real truth behind it can emerge. (In case it's not already obvious, I believe nearly all legends have some basis in reality).

Directly to the South of Fiji, 1600 miles away, is the island nation of New Zealand. It is here that we find another legend of a giant, man-eating Bird-of-Prey, strikingly similar to the *Ngani-Vatu*, known to the Maori people as the *Poukai*.

What makes this Maori legend both interesting and quite unique when compared with or contrasted to other, similar stories of giant creatures, is that the *Poukai* legend was almost undoubtedly inspired by a real animal.

Most scientists and scholars agree that the *Poukai* is actually based on a now extinct bird of prey: the gigantic *Haast's Eagle* (scientific name: *Hieraaetus moorei*). *Haast's Eagle* was the largest eagle ever known to have existed, and the largest surviving modern raptor on our planet, and astonishingly, it went extinct a mere 600 years ago.

The Haast's Eagle, attacking a New Zealand Moa

Illustration by John Megahan. Licensed under CC-BY-2.5

This fearsome predator had a wingspan of up to 3 meters. When compared to today's largest living raptor, the Harpy Eagle (*Harpia harpyja*), which can weigh up to 10 kilos, or 20 pounds, the *Haast's Eagle* weighed an enormous 33 pounds on average. They preyed on the also extinct, giant flightless bird known as the *Moa* (pictured above) and according to *Maori* legend, the *Poukai* were believed to prey upon livestock and children, and were able to carry away living human beings. Scientists believe that the *Haast's Eagle* became extinct when human beings killed off their only food source, the giant flightless *Moas* that once roamed the island.

It is my contention and theory that the *Ngani-Vatu* is in fact a surviving close relative of the *Haast's Eagle*, and that, in all likelihood, motivated by the rapid decline of their only food source, some of these ancient birds migrated north, in search of warmer climates, new food sources, or less competition from the humans. It's even conceivable that human travelers may have brought captured *Haast's Eagles* with them to Fiji. Whatever the case may be, I believe some of these giant raptors may have made their way north and ended up in the Fijian islands, where they were able to survive - and where they have stayed ever since.

The one factor which makes me think the *Ngani-Vatu* may be a slightly evolved version of their New Zealand ancestor, the *Haast's Eagle*, is that in many Fijian myths, these birds are believed to carry off adult human beings. This suggests that the evolved version of these raptors that I think may have migrated to Fiji, could be even larger than their now-extinct New Zealand cousins.

How could the Fijian *Ngani-Vatu* have evolved to become even larger than their already enormous ancestors? One possible answer is both logical and scientific, and can be found in the well-established biological phenomenon commonly known as island gigantism.

Island gigantism, and its inverse, island dwarfism, are examples of the "island effect" in biology, and there are many known living examples of this effect in the natural world today. Simply put, island gigantism means that animal species living on small islands can grow/evolve to dramatically larger sizes than their mainland relatives. This accelerated growth can occur within small island ecosystems, in which far fewer ecological roles are being filled. This decrease in filled ecological niches corresponds to a decrease in evolutionary competition to fill the few niches that exist. Often, on smaller islands, there are fewer large mammalian predators. Thus, the apex predator niche - being the #1 large predator - can often be filled by birds or reptiles. With a large abundance of food, minimal competition, and no known natural predators, these apex species can rapidly evolve to giant sizes compared to their mainland relatives.

The *Haast's Eagle* was already believed to be an example of island gigantism. But, if this biological phenomenon can occur on a relatively large island landmass such as New Zealand, imagine what might happen if these already imposing avian raptors transitioned to an environment of islands that were far, far smaller -- such as those found in Fiji?

If these birds could adapt to sustain themselves on a diet of marine animals, mainly fish I would imagine, then in waters of the island ecosystem that are so teemingly populated, they could access a nearly unlimited food source. This in turn suggests that the *Ngani-Vatu* could evolve to become far larger than before, not facing the same types of competition over a limited food source (the *Moa*), which had driven their ancestors in New Zealand to extinction.

Though I find it credible that these large raptors could have established themselves in the many uninhabited Fijian islands, it's also conceivable that they traveled to other, less isolated islands, in search of food or mates. Perhaps, every once in a blue moon, some might find their way to an island with human inhabitants. And, though by now they would have become accustomed to a marine diet, their former evolutionary instincts of hunting larger land prey, i.e. the New Zealand *Moa*, might kick in, and these ultimate birds of prey would obey their predatory instincts to hunt and attack large land animals. In this case: human beings and livestock.

I believe my friend had one of the only known sightings of this rare avian raptor in well over 100 years. If the *Ngani-Vatu* are still surviving in Fiji today, it's conceivable that any brave and intrepid explorer could, with some luck, venture into their territory to find and study them, and document their existence. The challenges of such an expedition would be significant, both financially and logistically, as the expedition would need a vessel not only capable of navigating the dangerous reef-filled waters, but also able to traverse the relatively vast distances across the largely uninhabited island chain.

Chapter 3
Sanctuary of the Mountain Yeti

The Tigers Nest Monastery in Bhutan

Photo by Aaron Santelices

In the heart of Asia, in the mystical country of Bhutan, there exists a very special wildlife sanctuary, created for a very special creature. The locals call it the Migoi, but to the outside world, it has a different name: the Yeti.

As unbelievable as this sounds, it's actually true. But before we delve into the mysteries of the Yeti Sanctuary, we need to take a closer look at the country where it is located, a place where one could truly say that there is magic in the very air.

Bhutan is a special place for a number of reasons. A predominately Buddhist nation, it sits on the border between India and Nepal, in the midst of the towering Himalayas. Any traveler who might have accidentally ventured into Bhutan, could easily think they had stumbled upon a magical realm that exists beyond the tethers of time itself.

Its stunning landscapes are dominated by high peaks, majestic valleys, jungles and vistas that feature Buddhist monasteries, which seem to have been carved out of the very rock faces of the mountains. The Buddhist monks who dwell in them are happy to live life at their own unhurried pace, and the locals rejoice in their favorite past-time, the national sport of archery. It might seem that the very land itself is enchanted with a serene essence, and one reason for this is that the government actually makes the happiness of its citizens its highest priority. Dear reader, your eyes do not deceive you, for in Bhutan, the "Gross National Happiness" is considered to be the most important metric, far more valuable than material yardsticks like the country's GDP (gross domestic product).

The Gross National Happiness is derived from four categories: sustainable socio-economic development, environmental conservation, preservation and promotion of culture, and good governance. Thus, it should come as no surprise that Bhutan is widely recognized as one of the happiest countries on earth.

Bhutan is also one of the few countries on earth that has maintained its independence since its creation, in the 16th Century. Bhutan is one of the few Asian kingdoms which has never been conquered by another regional or colonial power. (*NOTE: it was however forced to submit to Britain in 1865, after a short war, "The Bhutan War" which Britain basically won, and then forced the Bhutanese government to give up 20 % of its territory. Later, in the beginning of the 20th Century, Britain took over the control of Bhutan's foreign relations, so although Bhutan was still a nominally independent country, it was also partially controlled by and partially dependent on Britain. In 1949, Bhutan signed a similar treaty with India, in which it is transferred that dependancy*). In order to preserve its unique cultural identity, the rulers of Bhutan kept the country closed off from the outside world until the beginning of the 20th Century. Historically isolated from both its neighbors and foreigners, it was only as recently as 1974 that the government allowed tourists to visit for the first time. But tourism has been heavily restricted, and the government charges foreign visitors a daily fee of approximately $250, another factor which has kept the country and its culture isolated from other nations and their unwanted influence.

Bhutan is a constitutional monarchy, and held its first democratic elections in 2008, the same year in which it enacted its first Constitution, based on both Buddhist philosophy and a respect for human rights. Unlike other monarchies, most Bhutanese citizens seem to genuinely love and admire their King, whom they consider a benevolent ruler, and this tradition of respect for their religious and royal leaders has lasted for hundreds of years.

Putting all of this into context, it's understandable that, only in a country like this, truly closed off from the outside world for most its history, and featuring some of the most inaccessible mountainous terrain on earth, a large, bipedal, fur-covered creature such as the *Yeti* could exist in the present day with no one in the outside world knowing about it.

So strong is the Bhutanese belief in the *Yeti*, known locally as the *Migoi*, that in in 2001, the government took the unprecedented step of designating a vast, rugged area, in the eastern corner of the country, as the "Sakteng Wildlife Sanctuary" for the express purpose of creating a protected habit for the *Yeti*. This vast preserve, 253 square miles of protected habit, is closed to commercial development, and is also home to a number of other rare species, including the endangered snow leopard and the red panda. The two villages inside the Sanctuary, Sakteng and Merak, were only opened to tourists or foreigners in 2010, though ironically both are located in a protected area of what is already an already extremely inaccessible country. The Sakteng Sanctuary received a $700,000 grant from the World Wildlife Fund in 2005 in an effort to help preserve and study this unique habitat, and it is under consideration to be designated a UNESCO heritage site.

The locals of the area insist that the *Migoi* is real, and describe it as an extremely large, bipedal primate covered in thick fur. They believe the *Migoi* has phenomenal strength, and even possesses certain magical abilities, including the power to make itself invisible to thwart trackers or predators. Sightings in the area have been common, and when we consider this from a broader perspective, it fits in with a similar pattern of strange accounts of large mountain-dwelling fur-covered primates, in both Nepal and in neighboring Tibet. In all three countries, over many decades, hikers and mountaineers have observed strange tracks in the snow resembling human footprints but significantly larger, and a number of travelers have reported seeing strange bipedal creatures in both the mountains and the densely forested areas nearby. In Tibetan, the word "*migoi*" means "wild man" - and reports of sightings have not been limited to the Bhutanese or Nepalese. In one instance, a British alpinist scaling a large peak in Nepal, reported seeing what he described as a large apelike creature, that was apparently searching for food near his expedition's basecamp.

Artist depiction of a Yeti

Painting by Jonathan Dodd (@jonathandodd_draws)

All of these tales are fascinating, but they really all beg the question: can these enormous primates actually survive in the remote Himalayan slopes? And, more pertinently, does any hard evidence exist that they still do?

One of the more intriguing, and scientifically fascinating pieces of evidence ever unearthed in the field of cryptozoology, happens to come right out of the Sakteng Wildlife Sanctuary.

It was collected by a team of explorers which adventurer Josh Gates assembled for his TV show "Destination Truth" in 2009.

In every episode of this series, Gates leads a team on different expeditions in search of mythical or unknown creatures, often traveling to far-flung destinations in remote corners of the globe.

For the episode in question, filmed in 2009, Gates and his team travel to Bhutan in search of the Yeti. After a long and arduous journey into the vast Bhutanese wilderness via plane, car, rafting, and hiking, they finally reach the Sakteng Wildlife Sanctuary. They proceed to gather reports from local farmers and identify an area with the most recent clusters of sightings, where they will focus their investigations.

Though no definitive visual or audio evidence is found, members of the team come across a strange cluster of hairs, apparently snagged in the branches of a tree. The hairs are bagged and stored for later evaluation. After the expedition concludes, Gates takes the hair sample to a DNA forensics lab in Texas. There he meets with Dr. Melba Ketchum, a genetics scientist, who gives him the results of her analysis.

Dr. Ketchum states that she submitted a DNA sample gathered from the hairs found in the Sakteng Wilderness to a large international sequence database, which is used by many scientists and biologists to review, compare and identify 'sequences' from DNA samples, in the interdisciplinary fields which use bioninformatics (a field of science that develops methods and software tools for understanding biological data, especially when the data sets are large and complex). She notes that the sample, "did test very clearly on the human panel of markers," which in her view suggests it may belong to some kind of large primate. Gates inquires if it could simply be a human hair, but Dr. Ketchum informs him that a simple visual analysis establishes it is not from a human being, as the hairs are much coarser, and resemble horse hair.

Then, she says something that Gates finds borderline

unbelievable. Dr. Ketchum states: "Initial searches indicate that it's an unknown sequence. There are literally millions of sequences in this database, and we're really shocked to find that it didn't match any of the species exactly on the database."

Controlling his excitement, Gates calmly asked what would be required, from a DNA standpoint, to establish categorically that the Yeti is indeed a real animal? Dr. Ketchum tells him that what is needed is simply more samples similar to it, and that having enough samples to analyze will go a long way toward proving there is a new species.

Since there are no known large primates in Bhutan, as Gates explains at the end his TV episode, this clearly indicates that this hair sample must have come *from an unknown species.*

I believe this was a truly monumental discovery, and one that didn't receive the attention or recognition it deserved. I think we can say conclusively that Gates' expedition has proven that a hitherto unknown large primate is actually living in the Yeti Sanctuary of Bhutan.

I found another piece of supplementary evidence that I believe supports the Gates/Ketchum DNA finding: in 2018, the Discovery Channel broadcast a documentary titled "The Lost Kingdom of the Yeti." In this documentary, a team of scientists, mountaineers, medics, and Sherpas, launched an expedition to the foothills of *Gangkhar Puensum*, the highest mountain in Bhutan, and the tallest unclimbed mountain in the world. Before leaving, they are granted special access by the Bhutanese government to explore the area, since the entire mountain and it's immediate surrounding vicinity is closed off to all outsiders (pending special permission), as it is considered a sacred area, home to gods and deities.

After leaving the nearest city, it takes the expedition 6 days on foot to reach the foothills, whose extreme alpine environment is inhospitable to human beings. Fueled by reports of multiple discoveries of strange, apparently bipedal footprints discovered in the vicinity, the expedition's scientists plan to use environmental DNA, or eDNA. This novel method of DNA collection and analysis tests for small samples and traces DNA in dirt or water. Using this method, it is possible to identify what lifeforms are present in any given area, without needing to obtain a direct sample for each individual organism.

When they finally reach the shadows of the great mountain, they take a sample from a small pond, one of the few water sources in the area, and when the sample is analyzed, it is found to contain DNA from a creature that is "99 percent human." Since eDNA is thought to degrade rapidly, and since this particular pond had not been touched or "polluted" by any member of the expedition, the inescapable conclusion is that the sample must have been left relatively recently, within no more than a few weeks before the arrival of the expedition.

The analysis concludes that the DNA sample could possibly have come from a genetically unknown ethnic group in Bhutan, or it could have come from a completely unidentified primate species. Though this might not appear significant, a 1 percent variation is enough to differentiate one species from another, and even our closest known primate relatives, the chimpanzees, share 98.8 percent of human DNA. Thus, having a 1 percent difference is actually extremely significant, and is more than enough to postulate the existence of a completely different, and previously unknown, primate species.

This coincides with the findings from Josh Gates, because his DNA sample had "human markers," and although we don't know the exact percentages, it was clearly quite close genetically to the DNA of *homo sapiens*. This also may settle a debate that has raged for years, about whether or not the Yetis (and also perhaps the Bigfoot which purportedly inhabits the forests of North America) are some form of great ape, or a near human relative. These findings appear to indicate that the Yeti, at least, is a close human relative. In fact, this is not as surprising as it might seem, since modern humans (aka *Homo sapiens*) are known to have coexisted with at least 8 other early human species in the last 300,000 years, and furthermore, occasionally interbred with Neanderthals and Denisovans. So, at the very least, the notion of discovering yet another offshoot of our ever-expanding family tree isn't at all strange… but the one truly surprising aspect is that this new offshoot - the Yeti - may very well still be surviving and alive today.

Based on the discoveries of these two expeditions, I would argue that both of the DNA samples discussed in this chapter may very well come from the same species. And this species is none other than the Yeti, or *Migoi*, which has been observed, sighted, and spotted in this remote region of the globe for thousands of years.

Any intrepid or would-be explorers of this remote, beautiful, and distant Lost World, must come prepared to enter a region truly set apart from modern civilization. They must come with utmost respect for the traditions and ways of this ancient culture, and they would need to visit some of the most frigid and desolate areas on earth, the vast foothills of the Himalayas, where local traditions believe these primates live, in hidden caves and dens. And it is there, I believe, as they have for thousands of years, in one of the last truly unknown wildernesses on earth, that the Yetis await. It is as almost as though they might act as the sentinels of this unexplored wonderland, protecting and watching over their very own Shangri-La, the eternal guardians of a mystical, timeless landscape.

Chapter 4
The Oasis of the North

The Nahanni Valley, in Canada

Photographer Unknown

In the frigid cold of the Northwest Territories of Canada, since the dawn of modern exploration and even in myths and tales from the First Nation Peoples, there have been stories of a mystical oasis hidden in the frozen cold, a mysterious valley where prehistoric beasts still roamed. But according to legends, this paradise had a darker side, and its stunning beauty was tainted by a deadly aura: there were tales of evil spirits, malevolent entities, and even rumors that the very land itself had been cursed.

I discovered that this place is very real -- it is the Nahanni Valley, located in the desolate Northern Territories of Canada, a spot so remote that the only access is via boat or plane. Additionally, it is one of the most frigid and isolated areas on the planet. The Northwest Territories, an immense region with a landmass bigger than California and Texas combined, is only home to 45,600 people, with one of the lowest population densities on earth. Most of its rugged and beautiful landscapes are untamed, uninhabited, and often unexplored.

In 1976, the Nahanni Valley officially became a National Park, and was renamed "The Nahanni National Park Reserve," but the annual number of visitors to the park is still extremely low, less than 1000 people per year.

The First Nation inhabitants of the land, the *Dene* people, give us the earliest accounts of the pre-history of the Nahanni Valley. According to their oral history, in ancient times another group, the *Naha*, inhabited the Nahanni. The *Naha* were a violent and warlike people, who lived high in the mountains, and would frequently come down to raid the *Dene* settlements in the lowlands.

Eventually, the *Dene* decided to fight back against their warlike neighbors. A group of their best warriors was assembled, and they ascended into the foreboding mountains, deep into the heart of *Naha* territory. To their surprise, they discovered that, hidden beyond the peaks and mountains, was a beautiful and lush valley, irrigated by a river and featuring a warmer climate. The *Dene* warriors descended into the valley, observing what they believed to be the *Naha* settlements.

When they finally arrived in the dead of night to ambush the *Naha* village, and tried to attack, they were surprised to discover all the dwellings were empty. There was not a soul was to be found. It was as though the entire *Naha* tribe had vanished from the face of the earth. Curiously, the village campfires were still smoldering, the beds had been prepared for sleeping, but not a single person was in sight, nor did they ever reappear.

This shocking incident, the apparent disappearance of an entire tribe, was extremely unnerving, but the *Naha* were never seen nor heard from again. However, to this day, the area still bears their name, as the word '*Nahanni*' mean "land of the *Naha*".

This myth gives us a first hint of something unusual or sinister about the area. Though these mountains were said to contain a hidden natural paradise, the *Dene* never settled the area, and for generations they kept telling stories of strange beasts and of a malevolent presence that both haunted and guarded the area.

This might seem like a tall tale, but the eerie reputation of Nahanni Valley has continued for centuries. Since the late 1800s, it is estimated that 44 people have either died or gone missing in the area, many under gruesome circumstances, and the mysterious unexplained fatalities have persisted into the 21st century, when a pair of hikers on a weekend camping trip was found dead under mysterious circumstances. Though the official cause-of-death was listed as hypothermia, apparently there was evidence of gunshots, bullet holes in the vicinity, as well as signs of some sort of struggle.

In the late 1800s, as the gold rush flourished in Alaska and the Yukon, many trappers and fortune seekers were drawn to the Northern Territories. In 1904, a pair of brothers, Willie and Frank Macleod, set out on an extended trip into the uncharted Nahanni Valley. They were never again seen alive, and four years later their decapitated bodies were discovered, washed up on the shores of the Nahanni River by their brother Charlie, who had been searching for them. Then in 1917, Martin Jorgenson, a prospector, set out to the Nahanni in search of his fortune. Shortly after writing a letter claiming he had struck it rich, he too failed to return home. When searchers eventually found his decapitated body, they also discovered that his small cabin had been burned to the ground.

Because of these incidents, the area earned the dubious nicknames "Valley of the Headless Men" and also "Deadman Valley." Both incidents were widely covered in Canadian newspapers, giving rise to rumors of headhunters in the area, while also creating the unfounded myth that the Valley also possessed vast (and hidden) riches as well as a lost "Macleod Mine".

These accounts spurred other treasure hunters to explore the area, and in turn, many of them also went missing under equally mysterious circumstances. The few who made it back to civilization began telling new tales, doubtlessly embellished for their own reasons, that the Nahanni Valley housed a secret tropical paradise, where giant ice-age mammoths and other prehistoric fauna were still surviving and flourishing.

There may be a glimmer of partial truth to these tales, since the Nahanni Valley has geothermal hot springs and vents. This volcanic activity keeps the valley perpetually filled with mist, and also, fascinatingly, means that even in winter, snow rarely sticks on the valley floor. Geologically speaking, the Nahanni is a very deep valley, with a flowing river, and is heated by both seismic vents and hot springs. This allows the Valley to partially create its own micro climate, where entrapped heat makes the valley floor warmer than the surrounding snow-capped alpine peaks. It is thus believable that the Nahanni might literally be an oasis in a frozen region, a place in which creatures from a bygone era, or one of the planet's earlier Ice Ages, could have found refuge and survived for longer than other now-extinct species.

In the 1960s, more rumors of strange animals living in the area circulated. In 1964, John Baptist, a trapper, was hunting in the area with several companions. They saw a strange bipedal creature, resembling a neolithic hominid or Neanderthal, but short in stature. This being was extremely hairy and stocky, with a giant beard and dressed in a simple loincloth.

The following year, Frank Graves, an American cryptozoologist, launched an expedition to investigate the Nahanni. Along the way, Graves interviewed a number of the *Dene* First Nations peoples who lived in the vicinity, and they provided him with more details about the creature John Baptist had seen. The *Dene* called it *Nuk-Luk*, and believed that the small, powerful, hairy hominids were responsible for the many beheadings and unexplained deaths in the Valley.

According to *Dene* legends, the *Nuk Luk* (which means "man of the bush"), once roamed all across the arctic regions of the Northwest Territories, but now can only be found in the relatively small and warm Nahanni Valley. Frank Graves learned that *Nuk Luk* had been sighted close to several *Dene* settlements as well, and that the locals believed that, like the *Naha* before them, the *Nuk Luk* would roam the area in search of food. The *Dene* considered them to be extremely dangerous, a different species who had long been enemies of humans, and who now were fiercely protective of their valley. This was another reason why the *Dene* feared the Nahanni Valley, believing it to be the home of these evil presences.

While the idea of a surviving relict hominid, a near-human relative, is not at all outlandish, as discussed in the previous chapter, there is little more beyond the sightings, the legends, and the tales told by trappers, to prove that these beings exist, or ever existed. However, I find it fascinating that Frank Graves also reported seeing a giant wolf, which he later learned the *Dene* call a *Waheela* -- an enormous wolf-like carnivore that the indigenous peoples claim to have known and seen for centuries. Tales and accounts of the *Waheela* - which closely resembles the fearsome Dire Wolf (*Aenocyon dirus*), the prehistoric predator which went extinct 10,000 years ago --

are widespread, with reports of these hulking canines all across Canada, as far south as Montana, and throughout the Arctic circle.

American cryptozoologist Ivan Sanderson was the first to propose that the *Waheela* and other giant dog-like predators might be either surviving Dire wolves, or possibly surviving specimens of Amphicyonids, the extinct Myocene predators known colloquially as 'bear-dogs' because of their immense size and combination of wolf-like and bear-like bodies.

Early trappers and explorers also told stories of a terrifying creature in the Nahanni Valley that resembled a cross between a wolf and a bear. Though some claimed to have killed some of these beasts, none of the carcasses were ever kept or preserved.

While the foregoing descriptions sound surprisingly like a prehistoric Amphicyonid, I'm inclined to believe that a surviving Dire wolf is a much more likely culprit. First, because Dire wolves went extinct only 10,000 years ago, as opposed to the 7-million-year extinction date for the Amphicyonidae. Also, Dire wolves were known to occupy a vast area including most of North America and parts of South America. Dire wolves were larger, heavier and significantly more powerful than the largest wolves of today. Their heads and skulls were significantly larger than those of modern wolves or canines, with a broader palette and frontal region, which might account for some Nahanni reports of animals with a bear-like appearance.

The Dire Wolf

Illustration by Erwin S. Christman

    I find it quite believable that small numbers of these ancient carnivores could have survived extinction in this Canadian Lost World, seeking refuge in caves lining the Valley walls, and flourishing in the relative warmth of its micro climate.

    While it's now possible to visit the Nahanni Valley via charter or tour companies, it remains a very remote and perilous area. What makes the Nahanni Valley so interesting and also so scary is that, with all the strange stories and unexplained deaths, it is still virtually impossible for me, or anyone, to put a finger on exactly what is going on there. The fact that the Nahanni still has so many unanswered questions is rather chilling. I can't quite make sense of it, and though I have a gut feeling there is something out of the ordinary, and very strange about this place, I can't say exactly what. I reached out to an expert on the area, Hammerson Peters, author of "Legends of the Nahanni Valley," and asked him what he thought was behind all the deaths and disappearances. He succinctly summed it up in this manner:

    "Yes, the sheer number of unusual deaths and disappearances in the

area is definitely unusual. A lot of frontiersmen to comment on that fact have remarked that the area is especially dangerous, so the mishaps are proportionate to the hazards. But others have pointed out that no other wild region in North America, with the possible exception of the Superstition Mountains, has so many true stories of mysterious beheadings, which is certainly true. I personally don't know how I feel about the whole thing. It's definitely strange."

To all would-be explorers, I urge one thing in your investigations of the Nahanni Valley: caution! Do not underestimate this place, as so many others have before you. It is definitely a special region whose secrets aren't yet known, or proven, and warrants further study and expeditions before we will definitely understand the real causes of so many extraordinary happenings.

Chapter 5
The Lost City of Giants

Patagonia, the Land of Giants

Since the 1500s, there have been stories told of a Lost City, the resting place of the true wealth of the Incan Empire, overflowing with gold and riches. Explorers over the years have tried to discover this mythical city but failed. Perhaps notions of the fabled El Dorado come to mind – but no, the legend I write of is older, and perhaps the real inspiration and source of the El Dorado legend. Seekers of that mythical City of Gold (in Spanish, el Dorado means "The Golden One") have long focused on Peru and Brazil... But is it possible that they have all been looking in the wrong place?

This tale comes from one of the most wild, unexplored, and rugged places on Earth, at the southernmost tip of a continent: Patagonia. Since the earliest days of global exploration, this region has been known as the Land of Big feet, home to a race of Giants, the *Patagon*, for whom the area is named. The purported crowning achievement of this mystical race of Giants was their capital, sometimes called The Lost City of the Caesars, also known as the "Wandering City." Legends place this City deep in a valley of the Andes mountains, somewhere in between Argentina and Chile. The city is said to be overflowing with riches, flanked on one side by mountains laden with rich veins of gold, and on the other side, with diamonds. To use my Bolivian grandfather's phrase, this was a true "Shangri-La of the new world," and the legends of its inhabitants are almost as fantastical as those of the city itself: the last of the Giants of the Patagon, survivors of Spanish shipwrecks, exiles and refugees of the Incan empire, and even the Knights Templar.

To fully comprehend this legend, we must go all the way back to the very first stories about Giants in South America. This brings us back in time to before the dawn of the Incan Empire, to the mysterious cultures of the "pre-Incas" of great antiquity, whose origins are often debated, but in the case of the great Tiwanaku culture of Bolivia goes back at least to 600 AD.

This in turn, beings me back to my grandfather, Luis Hernán Tejada-Flores, who spent part of his childhood in Bolivia, who left when he was a teenager to study abroad, and who returned briefly as a newly-married man, after receiving a PhD. in Electrical Engineering from Caltech. But two years later, after the birth of his first son (my uncle 'Lito'), he moved back to his newly-adopted country, the United States, never to return to his homeland again.

My grandfather was a quiet man, and after moving to America, he did not speak much about either his family history or his life in Bolivia. But in 1942 he wrote a short article which was published in the Caltech Alumni Review. The article -- "Bolivia: Shangri-La of the New World" -- is an entertaining "read", and a heartfelt and colorful homage to his homeland, in which he rhapsodizes at length about the fascinating culture, beautiful locales, and his optimistic hopes for Bolivia's future. Though sadly he died just before I was born, other relatives have told me this article was the only one in which he publicly wrote about his native land.

Of particular interest to me was his fascination with the ruins of *Tiwanaku*, arguably the most important archaeological site in Bolivia, and one of the most important in all of South America. My grandfather writes:

"Like Tibet, Bolivia is a land of ancient and mysterious traditions. Centuries before European men discovered a new world, what we call Bolivia today was the cradle of the oldest civilization in this hemisphere -- one that was already obscure in the night of time when the later empires of the Incas, Aztecs, and Mayas flourished in North and South America. Little is left of this prehistoric culture, save what archaeologists have been able to piece together from the wonderful monoliths and ruins at Tiahuanacu on the Altiplano. Here, a race of gigantic men, more than eight feet tall, had built a city of temples and palaces and public buildings, of which the most interesting remnant is the Portal of the Sun, believed to be religious in its significance and astronomical in its construction. Tiahuanacu was already in ruins when -- as legend tells it -- two demigods were born on an island in nearby Lake Titicaca. These were Manco-Capac and Mama-Ocllo, who went to Cuzco and founded the Inca Empire; and modern Bolivia's Titicaca remained, until the time of the Spanish conquest, the sacred lake of the Incas."

The Gate of the Sun at Tiwanaku

What stands out to me the most about this passage in my grandfather's article is the assertion that these ruins were created by a race of 8-foot-tall giants, and the additional fact that Tiwanaku was already in ruins when later civilizations, including the Incas, finally discovered it. Although the ancient civilization who built Tiwanaku perished nearly 1000 years ago, there are still many legends and myths, told by the those who came afterwards, including the Inca - legends claiming that all of Tiwanaku had been built by either giants or gods or both.

I am particularly fascinated by the extremely advanced precision of the building techniques employed by this ancient culture. One of the "sub-sites" of Tiwanaku, *Puma Punku*, has bewildered scholars and historians for years, as many of its extremely hard andesite volcanic stone blocks appear to have been machine cut, with perfectly level surfaces, sheer straight lines cut in the stones, and seemingly impossibly precise drill-bit holes. No tools have ever been found at the site, and while most archaeologists, finding no evidence for any advanced tools, maintain it was all hand-carved, the whole complex seems to suggest a forgotten age whose inhabitants possessed high technology, and an extreme level of engineering sophistication.

Examples of mystifying stonework at Puma Punku

Photos by Wikipedia user Brattarb, licensed under CC BY-SA 3.0

Tracing the roots of the Inca empire, we realize that multiple pre-Incan cultures flourished long before the Incas, and in many of their former settlements, their ancient, ruined temples and buildings have been built and rebuilt, in multiple layers at multiple times throughout history. The Incas located many of their monumental constructions on top of pre-existing older foundations, which had a distinctly different architectural style. In some cases, it is almost as if the later cultures were trying not merely to assimilate but actually to imitate earlier ones.

In the 16th century, when Spanish conquistadors arrived at the imposing Inca fortress *Sacsayhuamán*, on the outskirts of Cuzco, the local population told them that the imposing stoneworks, which according to mainstream scholars had been built by the Incan ruler Pachacuti in the 15th century, had actually been constructed much earlier, by an ancient race of Giants -- and that the 'modern' (15th and 16th century Incas) were simply the ones who re-discovered it. Nowhere in the rest of the Inca empire, does one find the staggering complexity of *Sacsayhuamán's* architecture, with its titanic stones, the biggest of which stands 28 feet tall and weighs somewhere between 128 to 200 tons, stones which fit together seamlessly, despite their irregular sizes. So precise is the construction that, nowhere along the vast megalithic walls of the fortress, is there even room to fit a piece of paper between any of rocks (with the possible exception of the uppermost layer, which clearly was constructed by a different, later civilization). One wonders whether these ancient builders had access to some forgotten method of first melting down, and then literally molding the stones into a particular shape. To date, the construction methods of *Sacsayhuamán* remain a complete mystery, and while some archeologists still assert that each block was individually chiseled, they have no explanations for either the complexity or the precision of the final work.

A section of a megalithic wall of Sacsayhuamán, Peru. Note that the stones in the upper corners appear to be smaller and less precisely constructed

Photo by Ruben Hanssen on Unsplash

By the time of the Spanish conquest of Mesoamerica, the giants mentioned in myths, legends, and stories were nowhere to be found. But this is when another prominent legend arose, the story of *El Dorado*, the lost city which was known to the Incas as *Paititi*. To escape death, and to protect the relics and riches of their empire, the Incan nobility was rumored to have fled to a hidden city, deep within the jungle, known as El Dorado, the City of Gold. This is the story the Conquistadors purportedly were told, and for the next 500 years, first the Spanish, and later many European and English explorers launched expeditions deep into the jungle, searching in Peru, Brazil, Venezuela, and Colombia.

In 2001, a document was discovered in a Jesuit archive in Rome, dating from the year 1600, written by Andres Lopez, a Jesuit missionary, telling of a rich, gold-filled city called *Paititi*, located somewhere deep in a tropical jungle. In the subsequent years, decades and centuries, a number of expeditions were mounted in search of *Paititi*. Perhaps the most famous of these was led by Sir Walter Raleigh, who traveled all the way to the Guiana Highlands (located in present-day Venezuela, Guyana and Brazil), in search of the mythical city. To this day, the location of this fabled city is unknown, and in spite of many seemingly promising leads, explorers have never found concrete evidence of its existence.

The reason for this, I believe, is that the location given by the Incas to the invading Spaniards was, simply put, an elaborate ruse: a misdirection. In my opinion, the true location of *Paititi*, the so-called City of Gold, was a place the Incas needed to hide, a place hospitable enough and hidden enough to be secured, fortified, and protected by the escaping Inca nobility. And, most importantly: a place the Spanish would never find. A good location for the mythical city would be to the distant south, to the farthest, most remote ends of the Incan empire, perhaps in the far away land of the Giants: Patagonia. Similar to Machu Picchu, the mythical *Lost City of the Caesars* in Patagonia would most likely be located deep in the heart of the Andes mountains, but unlike Machu Picchu, no modern explorer has yet stumbled across an ancient city in Patagonia. Not yet, at least...!

While most people associate the Incan Empire exclusively with Peru, many don't realize that the Incan Empire also extended into Chile, all the way to what is presently the city of Quillota. The Inca occupation of Chile was relatively brief, beginning in 1470 and ending with the fall of their empire some 60 years later. Quillota is nearly 1,000 kilometers north of where Patagonia begins. This seems like a vast distance, but considering the Inca empire spanned nearly 5,000 kilometers, and that the Incas were skilled at building roads connecting all the settlements in their empire, the distance from Quillota to Patagonia could have easily been traversed by the escaping Incas, especially if there were preexisting roads. To make a long story short, the escaping Inca nobles could theoretically have reached Patagonia, a safe haven from their enemies.

The Spanish conquest of the Incas was one of the most brutal eras of history. The population of the Inca Empire was between 10 to 12 million in 1520, but fifty years later, in 1570, it had dropped to less than 3 million: an estimated 8 million deaths. Those not killed by the Spaniards were ravaged by disease epidemics brought by the European colonists. Given this grim backdrop, imagine the surviving Inca nobles - wouldn't they have taken any risk to preserve their culture and riches, and escape the brutal fate awaiting them at the hands of the Spanish? Including traveling to a remote corner of their known world, in the distant mountains of Patagonia?

But the question still remains, what happened to the mythological giants mentioned in the legends of the Incas, Mayas, and Aztecs? All three of these cultures had legends and myths of Giants in ancient times. According to Inca mythology, the giants were wiped out in a great disastrous flood, when the supreme deity Viracocha, the creator of the world, became displeased with them. This story is eerily similar to flood myths around the world, and especially close to the Aztec tales of a forgotten race of Giants who were killed in a primordial flood. But had these giants really all perished, or been wiped off the earth by the waters of a massive flood?

Supposing for a moment that the giant builders of old, the constructors of Tiwanaku, were real... where did they go? The answer, perhaps, has been hiding in plain sight. It would seem, by way of logic, or Occam's Razor, that they went south, to the end of the continent, to the land bearing their name: Patagonia. For if we scour the pages of history, the next known mention of Giants comes from an extremely unexpected source: the early European explorers and colonizers of the Americas.

The very first account on record comes from the voyage of Ferdinand Magellan, the first man to circumnavigate the globe, written by one of the few survivors of the voyage, Antonio Pigafetta, in the year 1522.

Pigafetta told a colorful story of first contact with the giants, whom he named *Patagons* to describe their race. According to Pigafetta, the giants were between 10 to 12 feet tall, and Pigafetta claims that after peaceful interaction, and winning the giants' trust, the Spaniards kidnapped two of them to bring back to the courts of Spain. But he then adds that both of his giant prisoners perished during the long and dangerous transatlantic voyage home.

Most scholars agree that Pigafetta greatly exaggerated the size of the *Patagon* giants, but the amount of his exaggeration is still debated. But ever since Pigafetta's account in 1522, the name stuck, and the region was named after his giants, and is still known to this day as Patagonia (a vast geographic region which encompasses much of the southern portions of both modern-day Argentina and Chile).

After this, the sightings of giant Patagonians continue for most of the next 300 years. In 1579, members of Sir Francis Drake's voyage circumnavigating the globe, report seeing natives of Patagonia that were 7 and a half feet tall. In the 1590s, two notable sightings occurred. The first was from Anthony Knivet, an English sailor, who reports seeing skeletons of 12-foot-tall giants in Patagonia. A second Englishman, William Adams, who was aboard a Dutch ship, reported a violent encounter between his crew and unnaturally tall natives. As late as 1776, rumors from the crew of English Commodore John Byron leaked accounts of having encountered a tribe of 9-foot giants in Patagonia. This account was denied by the Commodore, but at that time, skepticism towards fanciful tales told by sailors was mounting.

Another interesting story comes from the Spanish historian

Pedro Cieza de León, a conquistador who made it his mission to record the history of the Inca in his 1554 book, "*Chronicle of Peru, Part 1.*" De León writes that he was told stories about a group of hostile giants who arrived on boats made of reeds, and briefly occupied an area identified as Santa Elena, within the jurisdiction of the coastal city of Puerto Viejo. These giants, said to be four times the size of an ordinary man, constructed a village, and built a number of large wells and cisterns to sustain their great thirst. Their appetite however knew no bounds, and quickly they took to raiding the local populace, killing and murdering wherever they went. Eventually, these giants were killed off in what is described as a wrath of God event, destroyed by fires which smote them from the heavens, as punishment for their many sins. The giants were thought to have come from the far south, perhaps the furthest reaches of Patagonia. Though De León notes that this story may likely have been exaggerated, he states that he is inclined to believe the core events, seeing as how many people had reported seeing giant bones in the area, as well as the remains of the giant village, with great wells that still functioned perfectly.

Contemporary explanations for the *Patagon* giants have included outright hoaxes, embellishments, and suggestions that several unusually tall local indigenous groups, the *Tehuelche* and the *Selk'nam* peoples, might have been the so-called "giants." Since some *Selk'nam* men are recorded to have been over 7 feet tall, they would have towered over the relatively short 16th century Europeans (sadly, this tribe is now considered extinct, victims to genocide).

I would like to offer a different, radical theory: what if these "giants" of myth and legend and explorers' tales were indeed a real, but now extinct, hominid species, living in this remote corner of South America? They might have been an entirely unknown species, or one that would later be discovered in other parts of the world, such as the Denisovans or the Dragon Man of China (*Homo longi*).

One reason to consider the Denisovans, has to do with their skulls and dentition. Though only a few bone fragments have been found, one of the Denisovan molars is twice the size of a modern human's. The Denisovans are believed to have ranged over wide swaths of territory, and they are known to have interbred with humans, with some modern populations having as much as 6 per cent Denisovan DNA.

Another fascinating possibility is presented by the Dragon Man of China, and though only one skull has been found, this extinct hominid species must have been extremely large, even giant in stature, because their cranium was 9 inches long and 6 inches wide, significantly larger than that of *Homo sapiens*. The fossil-skull of the Dragon Man is 146,000 years old, but the actual dates of their presumed extinction haven't been established.

Imagine for a moment the idea of a great global flood, an antediluvian world event occurring in both Inca and Aztec mythology. Then further imagine a race of archaic humans who would have died out at the end of the last Ice Age, nearly 12,000 years ago, when (according to a growing body of evidence from ice cores, soil samples, and worldwide geological data) there is evidence of extreme flooding. One theory, the Younger Dryas Impact Hypothesis (YDIH), posits that an unprecedented period of climate change, which occurred some 12,000 years ago - in which worldwide temperatures dropped abruptly and a glacial ice age ensued - happened extremely rapidly, over a period of decades and not across hundreds or thousands of years, as had been previously assumed. According to YDIH, this paleoclimatic event, equivalent to a global environmental catastrophe, would have been triggered by the impact of a giant comet or asteroid. This would have caused massive global warming, by melting and vaporizing the two-mile high glaciers, which covered most of the North American continent at the time, almost instantly.

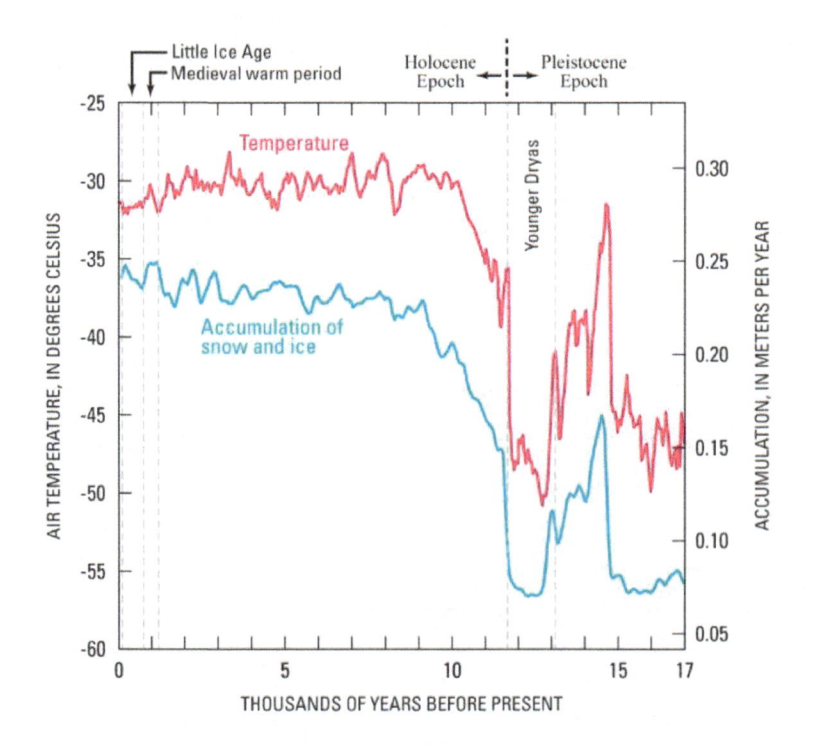

A diagram showing how rapidly temperatures and accumulation of snow and ice changed at approximately 11,600 years ago

Made by a 2016 official United States Geological Survey

    This theory goes a long way towards explaining flood myths found in so many cultures worldwide. It also coincides remarkably well with Plato's account of the destruction of Atlantis, which the ancient Greek philosopher claims occurred 11,600 years ago as well. It's conceivable that this global event laid waste to whatever civilizations existed at the time, utterly destroying them; the survivors would have recorded these events simultaneously in different parts of the world. In Egypt, for example, written records included both a flood myth, and also details of the fate of Atlantis. Many of these records were destroyed in the fire that swept through the great Library of Alexandria, but the accounts were conserved as part of an oral history told by an Egyptian priest, before the library's destruction, to the Athenian statesman Solon, who later passed them on to Plato.

Giving more credence to the notion of advanced ancient civilizations, one has only to consider the neolithic archaeological site of *Göbekli Tepe* in Turkey, the oldest megalithic construction in the world (megaliths being enormous stones, used to construct prehistoric structures or monuments). In an epoch when most primitive human societies were made up of nomadic hunter-gatherers, the unknown master builders who constructed *Gobekli Tepe* possessed advanced knowledge of construction, engineering, and architecture, and it has even been argued, of astronomy and early writing. Although some historians have suggested that this astonishing neolithic site was built by transitory migrants, a more believable conclusion is that the site must have been built by a large, highly skilled, and organized society. Using carbon dating methods, archaeologists have estimated the *Gobekli Tepe* was constructed near the beginning of the PPN, or Pre-Pottery Neolithic, some 12,000 years ago - or just before the global paleoclimactic events previously mentioned.

My theory is that the ancient populations of large 'giant' men and women who formerly lived in the Andean region - the same ones who may have built Tiwanaku - emigrated to the southern end of continent, for a variety of possible reasons, and ended up either dying out, being hunted to extinction, or assimilating with the local indigenous population. Did they create monuments and structures in their new home, the Patagonia Wilderness? Did they create a new civilization? And if so, where exactly did they live? Perhaps they built structures, whose ruins are still undiscovered - and of course, this brings us back to the tale of a Lost City, a city of legend which has never been found: the *Lost City of the Caesars*. Could this city really have existed? Could it have been erected and built by the fleeing Incas, on top of the preexisting structures and foundations that were built by the 'giants' of old?

The first written account of such a city, the mysterious city the Incas called *Paititi*, comes from the Spaniard Francisco César, who had sailed to the New World with the Venetian explorer Sebastian Cabot. In 1528, César led one of the first expeditions into the as-yet unexplored mainland of Argentina, and returned with tales of a land rich with gold and silver, and a large native population. According to some accounts, César discovered a city in the remote mountains, and this is where the legend was born. It's unlikely that the settlement César found could have been The City of the Caesars: it was probably one of the smaller Inca settlements of the period. But when news of his expedition began to spread, the name of the rumored city was changed from "the city of César" to the more mysterious sounding "The City of the Caesars." And this name change gave rise to a new series of tales and legends, as subsequent explorers mistakenly assumed César's city must be an outpost of the Roman Empire.

After this, there are numerous accounts or mentions of the City of the Caesars, too many to list in their entirety, but I'm going to focus on a few of what I believe to be the more important ones.

The first is found in a 16th century document titled "*Relación*" -- a notarized account of the adventures of two shipwrecked travelers who arrived at the Chilean town of Concepción sometime in the 1550s.

The two men, Pedro Oviedo and Antonio Cobos, said they were survivors from a shipwreck that occurred in the Straits of Magellan, from a Spanish expedition let by Gutierre de Vargas, the Bishop of Plascencia. After their ship was separated from the main fleet, they were trapped in the notoriously dangerous seas of the Straits, but most of the crew survived the sinking and reached the nearby shores.

The survivors, led by captain Sebastián de Argüello, trekked inland, eventually encountered an Inca settlement, and built a town on the shores of a large lake. The city thrived for years, but after killing a friend of the captain, Oviedo and Cobos were forced to flee or be executed. They trekked into the vast wilderness, and when they were nearly starving, met a group of indigenous people who identified themselves as Incas from Peru, and who offered them gold. Oviedo and Cobos refused the offer - all they really wanted was food - and eventually the Incas led them back to a road which took them to the Spanish colonial settlement in Concepción, Chile.

The important detail is that, in some versions of their story, the two shipwreck survivors came across what they presumed to be the ruins of an Incan city, laden with gold, during their trek through the mountains. Unfortunately, the full text of their account is presently in private hands, and only various 2nd-hand summaries of its contents are available. The document's current owner, the Martayan Lan rare booksellers of New York, value it at $12,500 at the time of writing this book, and their published summary makes no mention of any ruins, so for now it's impossible to verify the exact claims of Oviedo and Cobos. But, regardless, the document of these shipwrecked sailors seems to validate the hypotheses of both a Spanish city, founded by shipwreck survivors in the mountains near the Straits of Magellan - and also the rumored existence of at least one large band of Incas, down near the bottom of Patagonia.

The next most intriguing account is by Thomas Falkner, the English Jesuit missionary, who describes an epic journey he made in 1760, from Buenos Aires to the City of the Caesars in Patagonia, which he also calls the "Enchanted City." He claims the city is inhabited by Spaniards, and contains both beautiful temples and buildings made stone. In his account, Falkner locates the city on a plain near a wide river. To the west and north are mountains rich in both silver and gold deposits, which he says the Spanish are mining.

He describes the city as an "earthly paradise" overflowing with abundance, with all manner of sprawling vineyards, estates, fruit-bearing trees, and cattle ranches in the foothills. He also claims the local population is always healthy and free of all diseases, something he ascribes to the climate, and to the proximity of snowy mountains.

Another fascinating report was penned in 1776 by Captain Ignacio Pinuer, who was obsessed with finding the lost City of the Caesars, and who organized several expeditions into the mountains of Patagonia from the city of Valdivia. In his account, he claims to have received many reports from the indigenous locals of a hidden city of Spaniards, in the mountains. In some accounts, the city was constructed in a fortified location, looked like a castle, and was complete with moat and drawbridge, in an area rich in gold and precious metals. In other accounts, the city is either on the shores of a large mountain lake, or on an island in the middle of the lake.

In yet another report - a letter written in 1746 by Father José Cardiel, a Jesuit missionary who explored Patagonia exhaustively, to the governor of Buenos Ares - Cardiel specifically mentions the City of the Caesars, and insists it is located in between mountains rich in both gold and diamonds. He further describes the city as possessing both ornate houses and a church, and claims it was built on an island in a lake, deep in unknown southern regions of Patagonia.

When we take into account the multitudes of seemingly credible reports, mentions, and stories, from literally hundreds of different sources over hundreds of years, it becomes easier to believe that there may be an undiscovered city, lost in a wild, inaccessible and generally unexplored region. A city possibly founded by the Incas, or the earliest Spanish explorers, and occupied by them for a time -- a city entirely unknown today in the 21st century, whose existence has never been documented by historians or discovered by explorers. And this raises further questions... What happened to its founders or inhabitants? Did they die off or perish from disease, hostility, or some cataclysmic natural event? Did a handful of survivors eventually abandon it and migrate elsewhere, leaving behind mysterious ruins?

Trying to piece together so many seemingly unrelated myths, legends, stories, and forgotten historical accounts, we now need to try to see the big picture... to put together, as best we are able, the whole story.

Here is what I believe. In ancient times, the pre-Inca Tiwanaku civilization (aka the Giants) thrived in Andes of Peru and Bolivia, and built incredible structures. Then, due to some disaster or calamity, their society vanished. Perhaps survivors of this unknown catastrophe escaped to the south, to Patagonia, and attempted to reboot their civilization. Perhaps there, too, they once more constructed megalithic structures or buildings. But, eventually they either slowly died out, or were assimilated into indigenous Patagonian tribes, although remnants of their bloodlines may have survived until the year 1600.

This is where the official historical record helps us resume the tale, when some of the earliest Spanish explorers reported encountering people of larger-than-human stature, in many accounts, earning Patagonia its name. Later, during the colonial period in Argentina, sailing ships sometimes wrecked and sank in the dangerous waters of the Magellan Strait. Some survivors from those wrecks eventually made their way inland and stumbled upon the ruins of remnants of the lost cities, built by giant men. Some of these lost cities or sites may have been reoccupied by the local indigenous peoples... and assuredly the Spaniards also would have occupied them as well, most likely erecting Catholic churches atop the ancient foundations of the temples of previous cultures, or in the heart of their sacred sites, just as they had done with the Incas and Mayans. Building or renovating existing structures, the grandiosity of these hidden lost cities would have been exaggerated and magnified by travelers who stumbled onto them. They may have become safe places of refuge, too, for fleeing members of the Incan empire, or for rebels or outsiders fleeing the greed of Colonial Viceroys or the persecution of the Inquisition. And, though it's hard to believe, it is possible that some of the Giants of old still occupied these cities. I say cities, not city, as I am convinced there is more than one.

Though I can't conclusively prove any of the theories here, both mine and those of others, I would like to remind you, dear readers, that the region in question -- the vast fjords, mountains, forests, and jungles of Patagonia -- to this day remains one of the most unexplored corners of our planet. Navigating its bewildering terrain presents inconceivable challenges, and in large parts of the region, viable roads in or out simply do not exist.

Over time, I imagine the dilapidated ruins of whatever once was built there have been swallowed by the jungle again, and now may be so overgrown that their presence is not distinguishable in any satellite imagery. But I believe there are some key discoveries awaiting us, in the many mysterious nooks and crannies and corners within the Andes Mountain range, which span parts of both Argentina and Chile. Discoveries waiting to be 'found', and simultaneously preserving one of the greatest secrets of our time: the Lost City of the Caesars, or as I prefer to call it, the City of Giants, home of exiles.

Chapter 6
The Subterranean Realms of the Moon-Eyed People

The Mammoth Cave of Kentucky

In the United States in the second decade of the twenty-first century, it would seem there is almost no physical area or terrain left to explore or map, as cartographers and explorers have long since mapped every area of the country. However, beneath our very feet in many spots, there is a hidden, unseen underworld: vast expanses of labyrinths, passages, and caves which crisscross the ground beneath our very feet.

Many of these places, though they have been explored, are seldom visited or seen by anyone in the outside world, with the exception of the most ardent and daring spelunkers and cave explorers. We must recognize that our current understanding of cave systems around the world, which many consider exhaustive, is in fact surprisingly incomplete. Many cave systems and subterranean passages are completely undiscovered, and many more, even in well-established cave areas, are constantly shifting, collapsing, opening and closing.

One notable example, the Mammoth Cave in Kentucky, is the world's longest known cave system, and a staggering 400 miles of it have already been explored and mapped. But according to the Mammoth Cave National Park, as reported on the Department of the Interior's official blog, there is estimated to be the potential *for another 600 miles* of caves to exist, unexplored, within its system!

Even as recently as 2021, the Cave Research Foundation, a non-profit organization that has been involved in mapping the cave, announced that they had discovered an additional 8 miles of cave tunnels and passageways.

Though many people may assume that caves are a sterile environment that is inhospitable to wildlife, there are currently 160 animal species known to inhabit the Mammoth Caves, including rats, birds, snakes, bats, fish and insects.

Such relatively unexplored underworlds may be an ideal place for as-yet undiscovered species or beings not merely to exist, but possibly to flourish; and this potential becomes apparent not merely through modern and relatively recent historical accounts, but also stretching back in time to the earliest native American legends and mythology.

While many indigenous tribes speak of the existence of an underworld, or mention a hidden world of caves beneath the surface of the earth, there are also ancient tales that mention strange beings inhabiting these worlds, such as the *Paiute* legends of the underground giants, or the Ant People of the *Hopi*.

The *Paiute* legend of the Si-Te-Cah tribe describes that their ancestors, the northern Paiutes, had been at war with the Si-Te-Cah, a tribe of red-haired, cannibalistic giants. After finally defeating these ferocious enemies, the victorious Paiutes drove the remaining members of the giant tribe, the Si-Te-Cah, into the Lovelock Cave in present-day Nevada. One legend states that after their enemies fled into the cave, the Paiutes blocked the entrance and sealed it, lighting a fire to ensure the red-haired tribe could not return into the daylight.

The Hopi legends of the Ant People tell of a series of global cataclysms in prehistoric times, when the world was destroyed first by fire, then by water. In these ancient times, the Hopi people are said to have been saved from destruction by the mysterious and benevolent Ant People, who guided them into vast underground caverns, where they were able to take refuge and find sustenance. In some legends, the Ant People taught the Hopi ancestors both how to sprout beans, and also how to store their food in such a way as to avoid spoilage.

To me, one of the most fascinating of all these legends, and one which directly connects the distant past to the present, is the Cherokee legend of the Moon-Eyed People. Strangely, this legend also seems to connect us to the vast and mysterious Mammoth Cave system.

The Moon-Eyed People were reputed to be a race of short, pale skinned people who had large, round eyes with which they could see in the dark, but were very sensitive to sunlight. There are multiple sources and versions of the same legend, and most versions agree that the Moon-Eyed People inhabited the southern regions of Appalachia and the Appalachian Mountains. Many versions also claim that this mysterious tribe preferred to live inside caves, and only came out at night. Eventually, for unspecified reasons, there was a fierce conflict and war between the Cherokee and the Moon-Eyed People, and according to legend, The Moon-Eyed People were finally either eradicated or driven into hiding.

Scholars and historians disagree about the origins of this tale - did the Moon-Eyed People originate from Cherokee mythology, or was their existence invented or postulated by European settlers? Most historical and literary sources agree that different peoples have been telling stories about 'the Moon-Eyed People' for over 200 years.

One of the earliest written mentions comes from American educator and botanist Benjamin Barton Smith, who writes in his 1797 book, *New Views of the Origin of the Tribes and Nations of America*:

"The Cherokee tell us, that when they first arrived in the country which they inhabit, they found it possessed by certain 'moon-eyed-people,' who could not see in the day-time. These wretches they expelled."

To compound the mystery, there is a prehistoric structure in Georgia at the Fort Rock State Park which is said to have been built by the Moon-Eyed People. This 800-foot-long ancient stone wall was built into the side of the mountain, and appears to have once served as a fortification. According to some legends, it is believed to have been the one of the last places where the Moon-Eyed People defended themselves against the Cherokee during the war between the two peoples.

A section of the enigmatic rock wall at Fort Mountain

A 1956 archaeological report, the only accredited archeological survey ever done at the site, concluded that the structure "represents a prehistoric aboriginal construction whose precise age and nature cannot yet be safely hazarded until the whole problem, of which this is representative, has been more fully investigated." In simpler terms, we don't really know the precise nature of either when the wall was constructed, or by whom. Additionally, the construction style of the wall does not seem to match those found in any known Cherokee archaeological sites, or indeed in any Native American historical sites in the area.

In 1782, the former Governor of Tennessee, John Sevier, said that the Cherokee chief Oconostota had informed him that the rock wall had been built by "white men from across the great Water."

This seems to support a very popular theory about the Moon-Eyed People, which is that they may have been early Welsh explorers and miners perhaps members of the party of the Welsh Prince MADOC (full name: Madoc ab Owain Gwynedd), who is believed to have sailed from Wales to the Americas in the year 1170. Multiple landing places for Prince Madoc's expedition have been suggested, including Alabama, Florida, Newfoundland, and parts of what is now Mexico. Though the rock structure at Fort Rock has been attributed to Welsh settlers who purportedly accompanied the prince on his voyage - strangely, no other structures, or evidence of any settlement of any sort, have been found to exist at the site. One possible explanation is that the rock structure was part of a defensive wall designed not merely to repel opponents, but to last; while other possible structures of the Welsh immigrants, made of wood or less durable materials, would have rotted or disappeared. However, as it stands, this is all theoretical, at least until more answers are found, or additional archaeological evidence is uncovered.

One of the most complete and interesting accounts of the Moon-Eyed People comes from a plaque that was erected at the Fort Mountain State Park by the Georgia State Parks department, which reads:

"While some legends equate the moon-eyed people with the descendants of Prince Madoc, Cherokee legends tell of the moon-eyed people that inhabited the Southern Highlands before they arrived. These people are said to have been unable to see during certain phases of the moon. During one of these phases, the Creek people annihilated the race. Some believe these moon-eyed people built the fortifications on this mountain.

Other versions of the Cherokee legend tell about people with fair skin, blond hair, and blue eyes that occupied the mountain areas until Cherokee invaders finally dispersed them. Some tales said the moon-eyed people could see in the dark, but were nearly blind in daylight. Other legends describe them as albinos."

Finally, an anecdotal but strangely compelling argument in favor of the existence of the Moon-Eyed People comes from the book *Myths of the Cherokee* written by James Mooney in 1902. The Moon-

Eyed People do not actually appear in any of the documented myths and legends this book contains, but rather are found in the section explaining the complete history of the Cherokee people. It seems the Cherokee did not consider the Moon-Eyed People to be a myth, but rather a real tribe and a historical fact. After referencing the existence of a strange "dim but persistent" notion of a race of small, pale skinned men who had been there before the arrival of the Cherokee, Mooney mentions the account of Benjamin Barton Smith. After that, he references an account that he claims had been personally told to him by a man named Harry Smith, who was born in 1815 to a Cherokee mother and European father. Mooney describes Harry Smith's revelations in the following words:

"When a boy, he had been told by an old woman a tradition of a race of very small people, perfectly white, who once came and lived for some time on the site of the ancient mound on the northern side of Hiwassee, at the mouth of Peachtree creek, a few miles above the present Murphy, North Carolina. They afterward removed to the West. Colonel Thomas, the white chief of the East Cherokee, born about the beginning of the century, had also heard a tradition of another race of people, who lived on Hiwassee, opposite the present Murphy, and warned the Cherokee that they must not attempt to cross over to the south side of the river or the great leech in the water would swallow them. They finally went west, "long before the whites came." The two stories are plainly the same, although told independently and many miles apart."

It is very interesting that this account mentions twice that a mysterious group of people went west, and from present day Murphy, NC to Fort Mountain, Georgia, it is only a mere 70 kilometers west (and slightly south).

When considered in the broader scope of prehistoric structures, stories, and tales occurring in multiple cultures, and recorded testimony from individuals like Harry Smith, I think it is very plausible, and indeed likely, that a hitherto "unrecognized" group of people may indeed have briefly occupied the general area in question, in southern Appalachian region. But for those willing to seriously consider the existence of this mysterious tribe, "the Moon-Eyed People", this raises many more questions than it answers. What precisely was their origin? And what was the exact nature of their being, their culture, their society? If indeed they were diminutive and pale-skinned, and if their eyes had adapted to seeing in the darkness, *what* exactly were they? And, the big question of course... were they even human at all? Perhaps the Moon-Eyed People belonged to a long-forgotten or long-lost hominid species that had adapted to underground survival and living in darkness under the earth?

A lack of pigmentation is a common adaptation for cave dwelling creatures, and this aligns perfectly with the reports of the pale or white skin of the Moon-Eyed People. Their reported large eye size seems to fit the pattern of many nocturnal animals, who evolve larger eyes to see better in the dark. One logical consequence of nocturnal animals' increased night-time vision, would be an increased sensitivity to bright light, i.e. to daylight.

If we posit that an intelligent hominid species of subterranean dwelling individuals, who evolved an extreme sensitivity to bright light, wished to expand into more or newer territories, then an area such as the Southern Appalachians would have been an ideal destination. The Appalachians possess a great deal of both forested land and natural rock formations, not to mention that the Appalachian Mountains are one of the most cave-dense regions in the United States. Our subterranean hominids would have found an enormous number of natural caves systems, in which they could have built basecamps or constructed towns or cities — allowing them to live and evolve in security, before venturing out onto the surface world.

After their war with the Cherokee, most accounts suggest that the Moon-Eyed People were either killed, or driven from the land they formerly occupied, towards the West. If this tribe or species had been forced to leave the Southern Appalachians, where would they have gone? One obvious answer is that the surviving Moon-Eyed People would have escaped into the Mammoth Cave systems. The Mammoth Cave would have provided a perfect environment to take refuge. The vast size of the cave system would have given them many possibilities. Additionally, if the Moon-Eyed People already possessed superior night vision, this would have allowed them to settle in areas where their human enemies, whether the Cherokee or other tribes, wouldn't be able to find them in the relative darkness. The torches of Cherokee warriors would not have been able to illuminate large portions of the cave systems.

So if indeed the Moon-Eyed People took refuge deep within the shadowy recesses of the Mammoth Cave, what evidence exists to support their existence there, and could they have survived until the modern day? As discussed earlier, there may be over 600 miles of unexplored tunnels and caverns within the Mammoth Cave that have never been mapped or surveyed – which makes it at least conceivable that there might be a populated underworld beneath the known Mammoth caves. Perhaps the creatures that conceivably dwell in these nether subterranean regions, might at times venture up to higher levels or even all the way to the surface. And were that to happen, it is possible that normal humans might encounter them.

One thing which supports this theory is the relatively large number of anecdotal reports that the Mammoth caves are haunted, or at the very least home to shadowy figures, apparitions, or otherworldly beings. These reports are often made by visitors and tourists to the Cave, who claim to have seen, heard, or otherwise sensed strange things, or to have interacted with bizarre, ghost-like presences. Even the Cave's tour guides mention certain unexplainable phenomena, including the presence of shadowy beings who touch or inexplicably interact with the tourists.

Even more surprising are reported interactions with paranormal or unexplained presences, by members of the C.R.F. (Cave Research Foundation). One such report came in 2022, from Mark Wenner, a senior dive officer of the C.R.F., an experienced explorer who has for 14 years been involved in numerous expeditions to map and explore the Mammoth Cave. Wenner reported the encounter on the TV show *Expedition X*, and explained that a mysterious presence appeared to him out of the shadows, and seemed as real to him, as to the other C.R.F. team members who were accompanying him. Although not everyone visually saw something, all the team members maintain that they sensed, or could feel the presence as well. To this day, Wenner remains convinced that there is an otherworldly presence in the deepest levels of the Cave.

Dr. Patricia Kambesis, a professor of Geographic Information Systems (GiS) at Western Kentucky University, who runs the Cave Research Foundation in addition to being director of the American Cave Conservation Association, reported a similar eerie encounter on the same episode of *Expedition X*. Dr. Kambesis states that while exploring some of the deepest parts of the cave, she and her colleagues became unnerved after they sensed an unexplainable "presence" enter the area with them. Soon after, they began hearing rocks falling and unexplainable sounds in the vicinity. This spooked the entire team so badly that they immediately left that area of the cave.

Clearly, quite a few credible observers have experienced strange happenings in the Mammoth Cave. However, to really delve into the heart of the mystery, we should look more closely at several unnerving and as-yet unexplained phenomena taking place above ground, in the immediate area of Mammoth Caves. I am referring to the infamous encounters with, or sightings of, the Hopkinsville Goblins, as well as the Kentucky Goblins, as they have come to be known.

Turning back the clock to 1955, in the small, quaint community of Hopkinsville, Kentucky, which is only 80 miles distant from the Mammoth Caves, we find one of the more well documented and notorious cases in UFO history, which took place on the quiet Sunday evening of August 21st.

It began with a gathering of friends and family at the Sutton farmhouse, located between the towns of Hopkinsville and Kelly. Elmer Sutton and his brother John Charley Sutton were hosting guests along with their families, and in total there were 8 adults and 3 children present at the farmhouse who bore witness to the strange events that evening.

The sightings started when family friend Billy Ray Taylor reported that he had seen a flying saucer streak across the sky, while he was outside fetching water. None of the others present believed him, and they chalked his UFO report up to an overactive imagination.

An hour later, the family dog began barking frantically at some disturbance outside the farmhouse. Elmer and Billy Ray both ventured outside, and were surprised to see something unexpected — some kind of motion, and figures in an area of trees at some distance away from the farmhouse. As it was dark, and visibility was limited, neither of them could immediately ascertain what might be causing the disturbance. The two men, fearing the presence of intruders on their property, went back inside the farmhouse to collect their firearms.

While the rest of the family and guests watched in disbelief from within the house, the two men emerged onto the porch to confront the figures. It was at this point that they were able to clearly see the beings before them, who were advancing toward their farmhouse: short humanoid figures, perhaps 2 to 3 feet tall, with bulbous yellow eyes, disproportionately large heads, and gigantic bat-like ears. The beings appeared to have short and stocky legs, and horrifyingly long arms that reached down to the ground, with what appeared to be claw-like appendages.

At this point Elmer leveled his shotgun, and fired once at one of the creatures. The bullet knocked the creature to the ground, while also bouncing off of it with a metallic clink. This appeared to frighten the fallen creature and the rest of its comrades. The fallen being got to its feet, and the whole group took to their heels, fleeing into the surrounding woods.

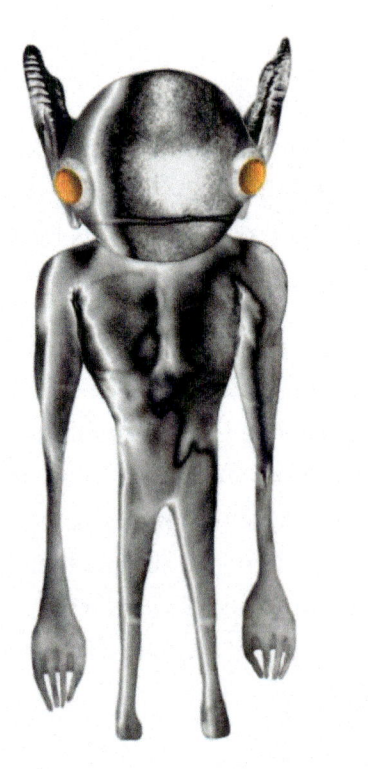

Artist's Rendition of a Hopkinsville Goblin, based of eyewitness descriptions

Artwork by Tim Bertelink, licensed under (CC BY-SA 4.0)

Over the next 30 minutes, the creatures reappeared outside the windows and doorways of the farmhouse. They began to scratch at the windows with their claws. Elmer decided to fire another shot through the window, and when he and his brother rushed outside to see if his shot had inflicted any damage on the intruders, he was attacked by another creature, which seized him by the head. A brief tug-of-war ensued but Elmer was dragged back inside the house by his wife.

Over the next four hours, the farmhouse remained besieged, with an estimated dozen or more creatures stalking the lawn, and trying to get inside via doors or windows. After this terrifying ordeal, the creatures retreated into the woods, disappearing as suddenly as they had appeared.

Early the following morning, the Sutton family went the local police station and reported the details of what had happened. The local police, who were familiar with the Suttons as upstanding members of the community, didn't know what to make of the story, but also saw no reason for the Suttons to be lying or to have invented such an outlandish tale. They were also concerned by the possibility that, somehow, the farmhouse might have been attacked by armed strangers. As a result, a total of four local police officers, five state troopers, three deputy sheriffs, and five military police officers from the nearby Fort Campbell went out to the farmhouse to conduct a detailed investigation.

Though many shotgun rounds had been fired and there was ample evidence of bullets fired into and through windows and doors, the police could find no evidence of any intruders, human or otherwise, in or around the property. Nor could they find physical evidence of any sort of unknown creatures having ever been there.

In the aftermath of this event, there was enormous coverage in both local and national media. The Suttons themselves, unnerved by both the incident and the ensuing barrage of publicity, moved away and sold their farmhouse. The hysteria surrounding the event culminated in an official investigation by J. Allen Hynek and the U.S. Air Force, as part of the now defunct U.S. military UFO investigation program, Project Blue Book. Project Blue Book eventually classified the case as a hoax, but did not provide any telling details or analysis of exactly how they had reached this conclusion.

There have been many different explanations as to what exactly occurred that night, ranging from outright hoaxes and lies, to being considered as a possible case of mass hysteria. Some analysts have noted that at a large gathering, many of the witnesses were likely inebriated and thus not in a very credible state of mind, and write the whole thing off as drunken delusions. Others have noted that in most parts of rural Kentucky, there are large populations of Great Horned Owls. The Great Horned Owl is one of the largest and most powerful avian predators in North America. They are known to exhibit aggressive behavior when defending an area near an established nest, and have been known to attack other raptors, mammals and even humans. Adult Great Horned Owls are typically at least two feet tall, and distinguished by enormous eyes, and large feathered ear tufts, characteristics which resemble the descriptions of the 'intruders' glimpsed by the Sutton family. They will use their powerful claws to attack enemies, grabbing on to their heads - behavior which brings to mind Elmer Sutton's account of being grabbed by his head. Great Horned Owls are imposing birds, and it is easy to see how an owl attack could have been misidentified as the purported goblins in low-light conditions, by frightened or inebriated people. For all of these reasons, I have to grant some credibility to the Owl theory. But, conversely, most documented owl attacks on humans come when the person has been walking near the trees where the owls have made their nest. For several owls to leave the shelter of the woods, fly out into the open and attack a human dwelling, goes far beyond the normal or expected behaviors of these avian predators.

For me, as for many others, this case is exceptional because of the sheer number of witnesses, who all reported seeing more or less the exact same thing, and who, over the subsequent years, have never changed or recanted their stories. It's worth noting that the Sutton family and their guests considered that the 'intruders' must have been aliens, probably originating from the purported nocturnal UFO activity in the vicinity which had been observed that evening.

While it is likely we will never know the exact truth, I must admit that idea of extraterrestrials makes for a compelling hypothesis, especially when seen in conjunction with the UFO sightings that occurred in the relative vicinity. However, like a handful of others who have researched this case, I actually subscribe to an alternate theory (one which some of you, my astute readers, may have already guessed!). Given the proximity between the Sutton farm to the Mammoth Cave, I think we need to consider that, if indeed these "goblin intruders" were real creatures and not a hoax, an inebriated mass hallucination or a deliberate misrepresentation, they might have originated from the bowels of the Mammoth Cave.

To take this theory a step further, I have to wonder whether these creatures might be one and the same as the "Moon-Eyed People" of Cherokee legend, if in fact my notion about them having fled, earlier, to the Mammoth Caves is correct. There are a small number of telling similarities between the Hopkinsville 'Goblins' and the Moon-Eyed People. First is their reported size: both of these entities are described as being very short in stature. Second, their nocturnal appearances and activity: both the 'Goblins' and the Moon-Eyed People are reputed to operate in dark and low-light conditions. Third, the large, bulbous eyes. When you put all three of these factors together, they seem to indicate that the two could indeed be one and the same.

In recent years, there have been reports of goblin-like creatures in many parts of Kentucky. Some of the more interesting arguments for the existence of the so-called Kentucky Goblins can be found in the first Season of the documentary series, *Hellier*, which features a series of similar and strange encounters with goblin-like beings in Hellier, Kentucky.

The first Season of "*Hellier*" focuses on the claims of a man who identified himself as a doctor named David Christie, who purportedly sent several panicked emails to a group of paranormal investigators, after which he was never heard from again. In the emails, he claimed he and his family had been witness to strange events, on a regular basis over the course of several months, when he said his property had been visited by short and pale humanoid beings.

Christie said he lived on the outskirts of Hellier, in Pike County, a coal-mining region of Kentucky. In his emails, he speculated the creatures he claimed to have seen were extraterrestrial in origin, and might have been coming from an abandoned mine. His emails mentioned other specific details, including human-like footprints, objects being mysteriously moved, closed doors opened, and repeated nocturnal barking by his dog whom he said sensed intruders. Christie also claimed to have seen one of the creatures, which he described as approximately 4 feet tall, with pale skin, and large round eyes. To back up his fantastic claims, he even sent photographs of strange, three-toed footprints, as well as what he claimed was one of the creatures, peering around from behind a tree in the dark.

Later, questions were raised about the identity of the 'David Christie' who had sent the emails, and whether or not such a person even existed, or if he had been using a pseudonym, seeing as how no one by that name had ever owned property in the greater Pike County. I'm not qualified to weigh in on those questions, but I will say that in a number of moments, the series, along with David's story, makes a compelling argument for the existence of small-statured, large-eyed nocturnal beings who bear a marked resemblance to the Hopkinsville 'Goblins'. As previously noted, there are a number of old coal mines near Hellier, and the state of Kentucky is one of the most cave-dense areas in the country.

If the nocturnal creatures described in Season I of *Hellier* truly exist, it is also conceivable they might have been coming from abandoned mines. If these mines were connected to a natural caves system, and possibly even to the Mammoth Caves, an intriguing corollary arises: could these elusive nocturnal creatures have emerged from a deeper, subterranean abode? In light of *Hellier*'s revelations, that would seem to be a possibility.

I am inclined to believe that all three aforementioned beings - the Hopkinsville Goblins, the Hellier nocturnal intruders, and the Moon-Eyed People - might very well all belong the same species, and share a common biological origin.

What is the truth behind the legend of the Moon-Eyed People? Is it possible these creatures still exist today, and survive deep in the hidden bowels of the Mammoth Caves? Intrepid exploring of new, hitherto unmapped portions of these cave systems is occurring every year. I believe it is only a matter of time until more concrete evidence about these once-mythical creatures is discovered, and subsequently revealed to the world at long last.

Conclusion

In the course of my own research and investigation for this book, I wanted, more than anything, to have taken you, my readers, along with me during my journey to delve into the most remote corners of the globe, into stories of places that lie beyond the furthest reaches of so-called civilization, places which are still intriguingly blank on most maps. And in so doing, to seek out the mysteries hidden in lands largely ignored or forgotten by most people today.

It has become evident to me that there are still many places left in the world that are virtually untouched by humans, and this book is really only scratching the surface of such areas. I chose to write only about those places which I could directly connect to stories of legendary beasts, or to tales and actual accounts of cryptids that inhabit these areas.

Of course, there are many more unexplored spots that I did not include (usually because of a lack of any evidence of cryptids), but which nonetheless are assuredly home to as-yet undiscovered creatures - places where the handful of expeditions to date have already uncovered a multitude of new species. Places such as the remote and almost completely uninhabited Star Mountains of Papua New Guinea, where a recent scientific expedition discovered two hundred new species. This expedition, jointly mounted in 2009 by *Conservation International* and the *Institute for Biological Research*, discovered two entirely new mammals, a dozen new amphibian varieties of frogs, and a multitude of never-before-seen insects and spiders.

While we're on the subject, another biological wonderland that is almost completely unexplored, is Cape Melville in Australia. Surrounded by mountains and a virtually impassible wall of boulders the size of cars and houses, the secluded rainforest atop the Cape was described by scientists as a "Lost World," when in 2013 a scientific expedition from James Cook University discovered three new invertebrate species. These species included the spectacular leaf-tailed Gecko, a golden-brown Shade Skink, and a cleverly adapted boulder- dwelling yellow frog whose brown spots or blotches allow it to blend in with the surrounding rocks.

These examples as just a tiny tip of the iceberg of the unexplored corners of the world that surely harbor undiscovered creatures which are bound to surprise and delight future generations of scientists and explorers.

Although this book may be thought of as the newest version of my own personal Explorers' Bucket List, any future expeditions to most of the places I've mentioned would be very difficult to plan without major funding; visiting them is still very much out of reach for even the most dedicated and enthusiastic explorers.

However, one thing that I have learned, is that one does not need to physically travel to the very borders of civilization, or to the most exotic of distant locales, to find actual cryptozoological mysteries to investigate; or for that matter, even to find places that are still largely untouched by humans, places that may have only been seen by a handful of other people.

Living in the most populated urban area of my home state of Oregon, it is a mere 2-hour drive to find myself in what is arguably the second largest hotspot for Sasquatch sightings in the world. I'm talking of course about the Mt. Hood National Forest, which boasts more confirmed Bigfoot reports than anywhere else on earth, except for the Olympic Peninsula of Washington, a few hours to the north.

In this vast forest wonderland close to my home, if one ventures far enough off the beaten path, or indeed, on any hike through a secluded forest, if one decides to wander off the trail, it is possible to be standing in a spot where literally no other human being has ever set foot.

The North American Continent alone is still home to vast areas of untamed wilderness. If one were to board a flight from San Francisco to Alaska, looking down from the plane's windows, there is virtually nothing but vast mountains and untouched forests for as far as the eye can see, stretching across three western states and part of Canada as well.

The world, as I see it, is still a much bigger place than I will ever be able to comprehend. There are so many more mysteries to still explore, and places to still investigate, that it defies logic and beguiles the imagination. I am hopeful that someday soon, or within my lifetime at the very least, one of the locations I've discussed in this book may yield an incredible, earth-shattering discovery: the confirmation of a cryptid, the rock-solid proof that one of these seemingly mythical creatures... truly exists.

Although I believe the yearning to explore and see what lies beyond the horizon and to discover new things, is part of human nature, another part of me also remembers some thoughts that were first expressed to me by Laszlo Barkoczy (the founder of the *Biocryptos* conservation organization), which I'd like to share and expand upon here.

Barkoczy points out that the related goals of exploring hitherto unexplored corners of the world, and making new discoveries, are intimately related to the need to properly protect endangered species. But, crucially, in order to protect an endangered species, we must know and verify that it exists in the first place.

The obvious corollary is that the governments of the world can only designate an area as a protected preserve, if they know that there are species inhabiting that area which need protection. In more dire cases, scientists and other concerned persons can only intervene or actively take steps to ensure the survival of an endangered species, if such a species is known to be on the verge of extinction.

And, make no mistake, all of the cryptids I'm writing about in this book will almost surely be highly endangered species, if and/or when their existence has been verified. The places they inhabit, the lost worlds, are more often than not among the most vulnerable places on earth -- places located at extremes of climate and altitude, and more at mercy of the potential ravages of both man-made pollution and climate change than many other parts of the world.

When studying cryptozoology, I am continually confronted with a strange and recurring paradox. The cryptids, often labeled as monsters, and in many cases reported to be ferocious, intimidating, and terrifying, are in fact among the most at-risk and vulnerable species on the planet, and perhaps among the most in dire need of our protection. It is up to us, human beings and members of the *Homo sapiens* primate species, to explore, find proof and evidence, and ultimately protect both the last remaining great wilderness areas of our planet, as well as the strange, bizarre and fascinating creatures, both known and unknown, that still inhabit them.

About The Author

Ben Tejada-Ingram Ingram is an author and researcher, with a special interest in unknown phenomenon and mysteries of the world. Through his social media brand "Anomaly Hunter" he delves into everything from the paranormal to UFOs, and explores all things unknown. He has always had a passion for adventure and discovery. This is his second book.

His first book, *The Last Dinosaur of the Lost World: My Search for 'Little Nessie'* is available on Amazon. This book chronicles his investigation of a mysterious but amazing story out of Venezuela, concerning the sightings of a dinosaur-like creature that was spotted on a real life 'lost world' plateau. From learning about this creature as part of an obscure and forgotten internet post, to tracking down every eyewitness on record and learning of its recorded history, this book chronicles the complete investigation of one of the world's most mysterious but amazing cryptids, the 'Little Nessie' of Angel Falls.

The book is available here (follow this link or scan this QR code to find it on Amazon):

https://amzn.to/34TNw8D

You can see Ben's work producing bigfoot, paranormal, and sasquatch investigations with his investigation team "Anomaly Hunters" on YouTube:

https://youtube.com/@anomalyhunters

Anomaly Hunters is a team of Investigators looking into every aspect of the unknown and every kind of bizarre phenomena, from bigfoot, to the paranormal, to UFOs, and more. Their goal is to produce high quality adventure and investigation documentaries, as we search for the truth behind mysteries all around the globe.

You can follow the ongoing investigations of Ben and his team of Anomaly Hunters on Instagram as well:

https://instagram.com/anomalyhunterx

Printed in Great Britain
by Amazon